NEW VANGUARD • 181

YANGTZE RIVER GUNBOATS 1900–49

ANGUS KONSTAM   ILLUSTRATED BY TONY BRYAN

First published in Great Britain in 2011 by Osprey Publishing,
Midland House, West Way, Botley, Oxford, OX2 0PH, UK
44–02 23rd St, Suite 219, Long Island City, NY 11101, USA
E-mail: info@ospreypublishing.com

A CIP catalogue record for this book is available from the British Library

Print ISBN: 978 1 84908 408 6
PDF e-book ISBN: 978 1 84908 409 3

Page layout by Melissa Orrom Swan, Oxford
Index by Alan Rutter
Typeset in Sabon and Myriad Pro
Originated by PDQ Digital Media Solutions, Suffolk
Printed in Hong Kong through Worldprint Ltd

11 12 13 14 15 10 9 8 7 6 5 4 3 2 1

Osprey Publishing is supporting the Woodland Trust, the UK's leading
woodland conservation charity by funding the dedication of trees.

www.ospreypublishing.com

CONTENTS

YANGTZE RIVER GUNBOATS 1900–49

INTRODUCTION

In June 1858, the Treaty of Tientsin (Tianjin) effectively opened the door to Western trade with China. The agreement was just one of several 'unequal treaties' achieved more by force of Western arms than by any Chinese enthusiasm for foreign trade. While Imperial China remained a semi-medieval land, many of its ports were now open to foreigners, and rivers such as the Yangtze (Chang Kiang, or Chang Jiang) could be patrolled by Western warships. The terms of the treaty were quite specific. The clause that governed the activities of the Royal Navy stated that:

> British ships of war coming for no hostile purposes, or being engaged in the pursuit of pirates, shall be at liberty to visit all ports within the Dominions of the Emperor of China and shall receive every facility for the purchase of provisions and the procuring of water and, if occasion required, for the making of repairs. The Commanders of such ships shall hold intercourse with the Chinese Authorities on terms of equality and courtesy.

Similar agreements were brokered with other Western powers. So began eight decades of Western naval presence in China, and the era of the Chinese river gunboats. The treaties included clauses that gave Western naval commanders the rights to 'protective action' and 'punitive action' – the former

The USS *Panay* (foreground), moored off Hankow, alongside HMS *Bee* and HMS *Ladybird*. Between 1920 and 1938 there was significant Anglo-American co-operation on the Yangtze, and the two flotillas often performed joint patrols, anti-pirate or bandit sweeps and rescue missions.

referred to the active preservation of lives and national interests, while the latter permitted retaliatory measures after a threatening or violent event, such as a gunboat being fired upon or the murder of Western merchants or missionaries. Gunboats were guarantors of Western commerce, privilege and safety, and were often all that protected the foreign enclaves in China. While our story concerns the whole eight decades of Western intervention in Chinese waters, these small warships really came into their own around 1900, and their heyday lasted until the late 1920s, although they remained in service until the start of World War II.

By the start of the 20th century, central power in China had all but collapsed, and local warlords often provided the only real form of government in many parts of the country. In the 1920s, General Chiang Kai-shek (Jiang Jieshi) achieved a nominal unification of China by military means, but Japanese imperial interests and the growth of communist resistance prevented him from achieving true national unity. The Japanese invaded China in the summer of 1937, and soon Shanghai and other treaty ports were overrun. That December the Japanese attacked the gunboat USS *Panay* off Nanking (Nanjing), an incident that demonstrated Japan's growing military muscle.

The era of the gunboats finally came to an end in December 1941, when Japan declared war against the United States and Great Britain. Allied support for Chiang Kai-shek's Nationalist Chinese government continued throughout the war, but the gunboats were only able to return in September 1945, after Japan's surrender. By then China was a very different country. It was ravaged by civil war, as nationalists and communists vied for control. Western warships still maintained a presence in Chinese waters, protecting national interests in the treaty ports, but the communists made it clear they weren't prepared to abide by the old agreements. In August 1949, for example, they fired on HMS *Amethyst*, which was damaged and forced aground. A diplomatic incident flared up, solved only when *Amethyst* ran the gauntlet of Chinese fire and escaped downriver again.

By the following summer, the nationalists had been driven from the Chinese mainland, and Western presence was restricted to the British territory of Hong Kong, the nationalist-held island of Formosa and the Portuguese enclave of Macao. There was little room for gunboat diplomacy in the new post-war world of decolonization, Cold War posturing and superpower geopolitics.

The Beacon Class composite gunboat HMS *Dwarf* was one of the first gunboats to be built for service in Chinese waters, and from 1871 to 1884 she was a familiar sight on the waters of the lower Yangtze, from Hankow to Shanghai.

Royal Naval gunboats, moored off Hankow during the early 1930s. The inboard vessel is the flagship HMS *Gannet*, while the remainder are (from left to right) the larger Insect Class gunboats HMS *Gnat*, HMS *Cockchafer*, HMS *Mantis* and HMS *Scarab*.

Soon the era of these gunboats was little more than a distant memory, something from a very different age, and from the far side of the world.

CHRONOLOGY

1839–42	First Opium War
1842	Treaty of Nanking
1844	Royal Navy establishes the China Station, first permanent Western naval presence
1850–63	Taiping Rebellion – widespread unrest in China
1854	US gunboat reaches Wuhu on the Yangtze River
1856–60	Second Opium War
1858	Treaty of Tientsin
1861	Royal Navy gunboats reach Hankow (Hankou) on the Yangtze River; warships of the US Indies Squadron reach Hankow
1861–65	American Civil War – US warships return home for duration of conflict
1863	French gunboat reaches Hankow
1866	US Asiatic Squadron returns to Chinese waters
1871	Royal Navy gunboats stationed in all treaty ports apart from on the upper Yangtze
1874	Gunboat USS *Ashuelot* reaches Ichang (Yichang) on the upper Yangtze
1876	Chungking (Chonqing) opened to Western trade
1894–95	Sino–Japanese War
1897	Germans gain control of Tsingtao (Qingdao) and the Shantung (Shandong) Peninsula
1898	British gain control of Weihaiwei (Weihai), and Russians gain Port Arthur (Lüchun)
1899–1901	Boxer Uprising – widespread unrest in China
1900	British gunboats penetrate the upper Yangtze
1901	French establish naval station at Suifu, near Chungking on the upper Yangtze; US Navy reinforces its river fleet, and creates the Yangtze Valley Force
1905	Russo–Japanese War – Japanese influence extended into Manchuria and Port Arthur
1910	Japanese annexation of Korea
1911	Chinese Revolution – overthrow of the Manchu Dynasty
1911	Hankow fought over by imperialist and republican armies – city changes hands

1912	Foundation of the Chinese Republic – collapse of central power in China
1912	Kuomintang (KMT); also known as Guomindang (GMD) founded as a force for Chinese national unification
1914	World War I begins; Japan occupies the Shantung Peninsula
1916	Collapse of the Chinese Republic; regional power assumed by warlords
1918	End of World War I; Tsingtao seized by the Japanese
1920	After using several other names, the US Navy redesignates its gunboat force the Yangtze Patrol.
1920–24	Various wars fought between rival warlords in northern and central China
1926	Wanhsien Incident – minor crisis in upper Yangtze
1926–27	Chiang Kai-shek's Northern Expedition – KMT advance north
1927	Split between the KMT and the Chinese Communist Party (CCP); abortive communist risings in Shanghai and Canton
1927	Japanese troops occupy Shantung Peninsula
1928	Chiang Kai-shek captures Peking
1929	Mao Tse-tung (Mao Zedong) assumes control of communist forces
1931	Major flooding in Hankow
1934–36	The Long March – Chinese communists escape nationalist encirclement
1937	Start of Sino–Japanese War; Japanese attack Nanking; Hankow becomes new capital
1937	*Panay* Incident – USS *Panay* sunk by Japanese
1938	Hankow captured by the Japanese
1939	Soviet–Japanese clash on border of Mongolia and Manchuria
1941	Japanese attack Pearl Harbor – commencement of war in the Pacific; Yangtze abandoned by British, French and Americans; Hong Kong captured
1945	Western navies return to China
1946–50	Full-scale war between the KMT and the Chinese communists
1949	*Amethyst* Incident – HMS *Amethyst* escapes from communist forces; Mao Tse-tung proclaims the establishment of the People's Republic of China (PRC); Chiang Kai-shek proclaims foundation of Republic of China on Taiwan

THE GREAT RIVER

When Westerners first established trading posts in China, they were only allowed to do so on suffrance, and in a handful of seagoing ports. After the Opium Wars (1839–42 and 1856–60), most Western powers signed treaties with the Chinese Emperor, permitting the establishment of permanent mercantile communities in a number of 'treaty ports' such as Canton (Guangzhou), Shanghai, Chinkiang (Zhenjiang), Nanking, Amoy (Xiamen), Foochow (Fuzhou) and Weihaiwei. A few countries established their own exclusive colonies – the British had Hong Kong, the Germans Tsingtao, the French Kwangchow (Canton) and the Portuguese Macao.

Of course, all these trading communities had to be protected. The Royal Navy first began patrolling off the China coast in the 18th century, but by the mid-19th century a permanent British naval presence had been established,

The waterfront (or *bund*) at Hankow during the 1920s, where the foreign concessions were located. Most of these impressive buildings belong to British trading companies. The gunboats anchored in the Yangtze are separated from the *bund* by lines of floating jetties.

based in Hong Kong. Dubbed the 'China Station', this force was created to protect British interests, subdue pirates and to 'show the flag'. Other navies joined them, most notably the US Navy, whose East Indies Squadron had a similar remit to its British counterpart.

For the most part, the warships used around China were fairly large – sloops, frigates or even larger warships, powered first by sail and then, from the mid-19th century, by steam. After 1858, though, there was a need for a new class of warships, small enough to steam far inland up the great rivers of China, where inland ports were finally being opened up to Western trade. Of China's two great rivers – the Yellow River (Huang He) and the Yangtze River – it was the latter that became the conduit for Western trade, and the place where this new breed of gunboats was needed most.

The name 'Yangtze' is largely unknown in China, where the river has several names. From its origins in the mountains of the Tibetan plateau (now Qinghai province), the river created from the cold mountain streams was once called the Hoh Moron ('Blue River'), but this Tibetan name was eventually replaced by the Dan Qu ('Marsh River'). It eventually becomes the Kinsha Kiang ('River of Golden Sand') before its confluence with the Min River at Suifu (Yibin), from where the river is navigable. Then it becomes the Chang Jiang ('Long River'), although an alternative and more poetic variant is the Ta Kiang ('Great River'). As the longest river in Asia, most Chinese simply call

A **THE BRITISH: HMS *WOODLARK* (1912); HMS *WIDGEON* (1919)**

The little gunboats HMS *Woodlark* (above) and HMS *Woodcock* had originally been built to support General Kitchener's campaign in the Sudan, but his victory at Omdurman (1898) meant that there was no need for them, so they were sent to Shanghai instead. They were shipped out in sections, then re-assembled, and by early 1900 they were flying the flag on the middle Yangtze. They were vitally needed, as until their arrival no gunboats had managed to pass through the treacherous Yangtze gorges, to reach the calmer waters of the upper Yangtze beyond. Western merchants there were vulnerable, so in May the two gunboats braved the rapids, and battled their way upriver to Chungking. They remained there for more than a quarter of a century.

Like her sister ships *Teal* and *Moorhen*, HMS *Widgeon* (below) was a slightly enlarged version of the earlier two gunboats, and was shipped out to the Orient, and re-assembled in Shanghai. *Widgeon* entered service on the upper and middle Yangtze in 1904, and she remained there for three decades, before being decommissioned in 1931. In September 1926 she played an active part in the Wanhsien Incident, as her crew attempted to recover two British-registered freighters from a Chinese warlord.

For much of its course the Yangtze flows through flat land, but above Ichang the river narrows and flows between the Yangtze gorges. This fearsome stretch of rapids, shoals and seasonally changeable river levels divided the upper and lower Yangtze.

it Kiang or Jiang, meaning 'The River'. 'Yangtze' probably derives from Yang Tzu, the old name for the river city of Chinkiang. 'Yangtze' is simply a foreign misinterpretation, the Westerners applying the title to the whole river, although it could also be an extension of the word *yang*, meaning 'ocean'. In any case, only Westerners called this great river the Yangtze.

The Yangtze is more than 3,900 miles long, although its exact length is hard to measure – the river keeps growing as silt is carried downstream and deposited at the mouth of the Yangtze estuary. Every year around 30 yards of silt turns into mudflats, pushing the mouth of the river into the East China Sea. Over the centuries this effect has created a great alluvial plain, which has been settled and farmed, and used as a haven for pirates. The first traces of the Yangtze can be seen almost 100 miles from its mouth, where the sea becomes discoloured by the sediment. The river itself is brownish-yellow, the colour caused by the sediment and aided by human effluence. For much of its lower course it meanders through a low-lying flood plain dominated by rice paddies and swampland, interspersed with settlements varying from small villages to major cities.

The river's navigable course has been described as resembling a widely splayed letter 'W', with the river port of Hankow – one of the triple cities that make up Wuhan – at its apex, some 600 miles from the sea. Downriver the river is fed by the fresh waters of Poyang Lake, before curving up again towards Nanking and Chinkiang. From there it flows in a south-easterly direction past Shanghai and down towards the open sea. Above Hankow the left half of the 'W' extends shakily for 370 miles to Ichang, which marks the start of the navigable upper river. At the bottom of this 'W' lies a tributary called the Xiang that flows into Tung Ting (Dong Ting) Lake, and leads to another treaty city – Changsha, the capital of Hunan province. There an ancient canal connected the Xiang with Canton on the Pearl River, but by the start of the 20th century a railway linked Canton to Changsha, before reaching Wuchang, on the south bank of the Yangtze opposite Hankow. From Hankow another railway line ran north to Peking.

Beyond Ichang the mountains close in, creating the spectacular Yangtze gorges, and a navigable hazard in the form of rapids and fallen boulders. Another hazard is the water level, which can vary by 50ft or more overnight, leaving ships hard aground and turning the river into a foaming cataract. Beyond this difficult but beautiful stretch of water, the river continues upstream to the last inland treaty port of Chungking, 430 miles above Ichang, and a staggering 1,500 miles from the sea. There the height of the river can vary by as much as 100ft, depending on the conditions and the season. The navigable river actually extends for a further 200 miles to Suifu, but as this

In 1931 the city of Hankow was flooded when the Yangtze overflowed its banks. While thousands died, and the city was badly damaged, a British gunboat officer described the scene in the flooded city as reminiscent of the Henley Regatta.

wasn't a treaty port Western gunboats rarely made the trip that far upriver, although the French did establish a small naval base there in the early 1900s.

For the best part of eight decades, from 1858 until 1941, these 1,700 miles of river were patrolled by Western gunboats, and occasionally by Chinese warships, owned by emperors, nationalist factions or local warlords. Given Hankow's geographical location, it was inevitable that the city would become the centre of gunboat activity on the river, although they occasionally ventured downriver to Shanghai, where the Western maritime powers stationed larger and more formidable warships. These gunboats shared the river with thousands of other vessels, from the large steamships owned by Western shipping companies to the more mundane junks and sampans, whose owners earned their livelihood on the great river.

The Yangtze has been described as the 'Golden Waterway' of China, dividing north from south, but linking the country through riverine trade. To the ancient Chinese, the river was the home of a great underwater dragon, whose changes in mood explained all river disasters, from shipwreck to flooding, stranding or piracy. The job of the Yangtze gunboats was to keep an eye on this great dragon, and to protect Westerners from its wrath.

PATROLLING THE YANGTZE

The Early Years, 1858–99

The story of the Yangtze gunboats really starts with Henry Temple, Lord Palmerston. In 1850, as the British Foreign Secretary, he sent a naval squadron to the Aegean, to intervene in Greek affairs. His 'gunboat diplomacy' worked well, and when he became Prime Minister five years later he was willing to repeat the tactic in China, where a new crisis was brewing. Despite its name, the Second Opium War (1856–60) was less about opium than about trade, and Palmerston used the navy to achieve his war aims – commercial access to China, including the removal of tax restrictions on Western goods. Western victories over China led to the Treaty of Tientsin of June 1858, to which Britain, France, Russia and the United States were signatories. Under its terms remaining trade restrictions were removed, and Western merchants were allowed to establish trading posts in Nanking, Hankow and several smaller ports on the Yangtze River. In effect, the treaty opened up the Chinese hinterland to foreign commerce.

USS *Monocacy* was a double-ended sidewheel steamer, laid down during the American Civil War. One of the first American Yangtze gunboats, she served on the river from 1866 until 1903, even though she was singularly unsuited to her role.

The foreign merchants needed to be protected, so a clause in the treaty allowed Western warships to navigate the Yangtze, penetrating into the very heart of China and dominating its largest river. The first Westerners to venture up the river were British explorers, but gunboats followed in their wake. In February 1861, Rear-Admiral James Hope led a British flotilla up the Yangtze as far as Hankow. These warships were soon followed by merchantmen, and within a decade Hankow, like Wuhu and Chinkiang further downstream had become a bustling international community, where Western merchants and sailors lived and worked deep inside China, 600 miles from the open sea. A small American flotilla followed the British to Hankow, but when news reached them of the outbreak of the American Civil War (1861–65) they returned home, leaving the Europeans to safeguard Western interests on the river. The first French warship, the *Kien Chan*, reached Hankow two years later, and other nationalities would follow.

The US Navy returned in 1866, but it lacked the ships to make its presence felt. In 1871 the USS *Benicia* made a goodwill tour up the Yangtze, to find British warships in every port. This presence reflected the British policy of stationing at least one gunboat in every port where there was a British consul, to protect life and property. Still, by the end of 1866 the Americans had two gunboats stationed on the Yangtze – *Monocacy* and *Ashuelot* – but it would be three decades before the US Navy really began to make its presence felt.

B **THE AMERICANS: USS *VILLALOBOS* (1914); USS *PALOS* (1921)**

During the Spanish–American War of 1898, several Spanish gunboats were captured in the Philippines and elsewhere, and some of them were commissioned into the US Navy. Of these, the USS *Elcano*, the USS *Quiros* and the USS *Villalobos* (above) were sent to the Yangtze in 1903, and spent most of their remaining service lives there. During her quarter of a century on the Yangtze the USS *Villalobos* fought pirates and bandits, escorted American-registered ships and offered protection to American merchants and missionaries. As late as 1927 – a year before she was decommissioned– *Villalobos* was used to protect American businesses in Nanking from marauding Chinese troops.

The USS *Palos* (below) and her sister ship USS *Monocacy* – the second *Monocacy* to serve on the Yangtze – ware launched in Shanghai in 1914, shortly before the outbreak of World War I. The two gunboats were powerful enough to navigate the rapids of the Yangtze gorges, and they demonstrated this capability on their first patrol by reaching Chungking, 1,300 miles from the open sea. They were reliable, but not particularly suited to conditions on the Yangtze. By the 1920s the *Palos* was relegated to the lower river, and she was finally decommissioned in 1937.

The Heyday of the Yangtze Gunboats, 1900–20

While ocean-going gunboats could be used on the lower and middle Yangtze, China Station commanders demanded gunboats that could also pass through the gorges to reach the upper river. The result was HMS *Woodlark* and HMS *Woodcock*, built in 1897 for service on the River Nile. The British victory over the Mahdists at Omdurman (1898) made them surplus to requirements, so they were shipped to the Far East instead. They were ready for service in August 1898, and in March 1900 they successfully navigated the Yangtze gorges, and becoming the first Western gunboats to reach Chungking, on the upper river. They remained there for the best part of three decades, protecting British interests, and surveying the upper Yangtze.

In 1900 two new American warships appeared – the USS *Helena* and the USS *Wilmington*. They were soon followed by a motley collection of older US gunboats, all of which had once flown the flag of Spain. The *Elcano*, *Samar*, *Quinto* and *Villalobos* became regular sights on the river, and would remain on the Yangtze for quarter of a century, until a new generation of gunboats replaced them. Other nations sent their ships too. The French vessel *Olry* reached Chungking in November 1901, making her the largest Western gunboat to navigate the gorges. Like *Woodcock* and *Woodlark*, she remained on the upper Yangtze, based on the newly founded French naval station at Suifu, a non-treaty port even further upriver than Chungking. Another French gunboat – the *Takiang* – arrived to patrol the middle and lower Yangtze, and in 1910 she was reinforced by the *Doudart de Lagrée*, which could operate anywhere on the river from Suifu to Shanghai.

Another newcomer was Imperial Germany. In 1897 it gained control of Tsingtao in Shantung province, on the coast of the China Sea. That year the gunboat *Wolf* was stationed there as guardship. By 1901, the gunboats *Vorwärts* and *Vaterland* had arrived on the Yangtze, and patrolled the shallow waters of Poyang Lake. The larger gunboats *Jaguar*, *Tiger*, *Luchs* and *Iltis* were limited to the lower Yangtze. The ageing *Vorwärts* was decommissioned in 1910, when she was replaced by the more modern gunboat *Otter*. Tsingtao, however, remained the real centre of German political and mercantile interests in China, and the home port of Germany's Asiatic Squadron.

Then there were the Japanese. As a result of their victory in the Sino–Japanese War (1894–95), they gained trading concessions in China, and Japanese warships began appearing in the treaty ports. Between 1900 and 1920, the number of Japanese civilians in China quadrupled. By then the Japanese had become the largest foreign contingent in Shanghai, and from 1903 their gunboats patrolled the Yangtze from Hankow down to Shanghai.

HMS *Woodlark* was built in Britain for service on the Nile, but in 1898 she was sent to the Yangtze instead. She was shipped in sections – the numbers on the hull were designed to assist her re-assembly.

Japan maintained gunboats on the Yangtze from 1906 onwards, but this force was substantially reinforced during the late 1920s. The IJNS *Atami* was a modified Seta Class gunboat, and served on the river from 1930 until her surrender in 1945.

After Japan's victory in the Russo–Japanese War (1904–05) Japanese warships appeared on the Yangtze in greater numbers, as Japanese troops occupied Korea and Manchuria. For the next four decades, Japan would be the dominant regional power in the Far East, and its gunboats would be an ever more frequent sight on the river. In 1911 the gunboat *Fushimi* reached the upper river, but for the most part the Japanese sphere of influence remained the lower Yangtze.

In 1911 China was torn apart by revolution, brought about by widespread exasperation with imperial rule. Republicanism swept the country, and armed risings turned into national revolution. On the Yangtze, rioting broke out in Hankow, Nanking, Shanghai and other treaty ports, and law and order collapsed. In October 1911 the situation in Hankow had grown so turbulent that 20 gunboats were moored in the river – six British, four German, three American, three Japanese, two Russian, one French and one Austro-Hungarian. While the native city burned, international naval landing parties protected the foreign quarter.

The next upheaval came in August 1914, and the outbreak of World War I (1914–18). China was a neutral country, so any combatant gunboat that was unable to leave the river faced internment. Some warships like HMS *Nightingale* or SMS *Otter* were interned voluntarily, as their crews were needed elsewhere. Other gunboats like the French *Doudart de Lagrée* raced down the river to the open sea. Shanghai was in turmoil, as many Europeans tried to head home, while Hong Kong turned into a bustling staging post for Entente warships. For its part, the powerful German Asiatic Squadron slipped out of Tsingtao and headed towards the Pacific on the first leg of a voyage that would take it to Cape Coronel and the Falklands. The Japanese captured Tsingtao soon after the German departure, and overran the Shantung peninsula.

The sister of the second USS *Monocacy*, USS *Palos* was originally designed for service on the Great Lakes, but was assembled in Shanghai and served on the Yangtze instead. *Palos* became the first American warship to navigate the upper Yangtze.

The purpose-built river gunboat USS *Helena* arrived on the Yangtze in late 1900, and until the 1920s she and her sister ship USS *Wilmington* took it in turns to serve as the American flagship on the river, based in Hankow.

Within weeks, the Yangtze was almost devoid of gunboats. Only the US Navy's newly-designated Yangtze Valley Force remained, and its ships took on the task of protecting all Western interests on the river, whether American or European. A snapshot of their deployment in April 1916 shows how the Americans tried to cover the entire river. *Monocacy* was in Chungking on the upper river, *Palos* was visiting the Xian and Tung Ting Lake, while *Villalobos* was anchored off Hankow. Further downstream the *Samar* was off Kiukiang (Jiujiang), *Quiros* lay off Nanking and the flagship *Helena* was moored off Shanghai.

When the United States entered the war in April 1917, these gunboats were interned at Shanghai, but this period was short-lived, as China joined the conflict that August on the Entente side. The gunboats were re-crewed, and posted at intervals from Changsha to Shanghai.

The coming of peace in November 1918 ushered in a new era on the Yangtze. With the exception of Germany and Russia the Western powers returned, as did their merchants and missionaries. It was business as usual, except that this time the Western powers were less inclined to tolerate Chinese lawlessness, and more willing to impose law and order by force. The war years had seen a decline in stability within China, and by 1919 the country was divided into small fiefdoms run by rival Chinese warlords. Given this semi-anarchic state it seemed natural that gunboat captains would maintain order on the river, and in the treaty ports. Another change was that the US Navy had moved up in the international rankings, the improvement in status reflected by its positioning in the moorings off Shanghai, between the British and the Japanese.

In 1920, the Yangtze Valley Force was re-designated the Yangtze Patrol, a name the American gunboat force would retain until World War II. There was also a high level of Anglo-American cooperation during this period. While the crews of the gunboats might fight each other in the bars of Hankow

C **HMS *COCKCHAFER* AT WANHSIEN, 1926**

In August 1926, a sampan filled with Chinese soldiers capsized during an illegal attempt to board the British-flagged river steamer SS *Wanliu*. This incident sparked a confrontation between the British and General Yang, the local Chinese warlord. Yang's men seized two more British ships, the SS *Wanhsien* and the SS *Wantung*, moored off Wanhsien on the upper Yangtze. Lieutenant-Commander Acheson of *Cockchafer* lacked the manpower to deal with the situation, so the SS *Kiawo* was sent upriver from Hankow, carrying a naval boarding party. On the evening of 6 September, the *Kiawo* reached Wanhsien, and troops boarded the *Wanhsien*. The Chinese were waiting, and opened up with rifles and machine-guns. Despite the heavy fire, the attackers rescued the British hostages, then withdrew to the *Kiawo*. The hostages from the *Wantung* also escaped in the confusion, and swam to safety. During the assault *Cockchafer* and a new arrival – HMS *Widgeon* – exchanged fire with the Chinese on the shore. The two British ships then slipped away to safety, having suffered seven casualties. The plate shows HMS *Cockchafer* in the thick of the action, supported by *Widgeon*. In the background the *Kiawo* can be seen heading back downriver with the rescued hostages.

The second USS *Monocacy* to serve on the Yangtze, this vessel was slightly better suited to the role than her predecessor, but like her sister ship *Palos* she was plagued by mechanical problems, although she remained in service until 1939.

or Shanghai, they demonstrated a singular solidarity on the river. In fact, on the upper Yangtze the USS *Monocacy* and USS *Palos* operated alongside HMS *Teal* and HMS *Widgeon*, jointly protecting Anglo-American interests, and supporting each other by sharing supplies, duties and even crewmen.

The Years of Turmoil, 1921–30

During the 1920s, the political situation in China was chaotic, and instances of banditry and piracy were on the rise. Increasingly, river steamers were escorted past known trouble spots, and gunboats were stationed in the treaty ports, ready to intervene if rioting broke out. For instance, in July 1920 eight warships lay off Hankow: the light cruiser HMS *Hawkins* and seven gunboats, of which three were British, two American, one Italian and one French. The Western powers were determined that however unstable China might be, their own communities would be protected.

The situation would soon become a lot worse. During the early 1920s, the KMT developed a power base in Canton and surrounding Kwangtung (Guangdong) province. The political affiliations of the KMT were ambivalent, but the party maintained ties with the Soviet Union, and was generally viewed by Westerners as being both revolutionary and anti-Western. In 1925 Chiang Kai-shek assumed the leadership of the KMT, and began planning a military campaign of unification, aiming to strike north into the territory ruled by the warlords.

At that time, the Yangtze and its major tributary, the Xiang, lay within the territory of three rival warlords. Wu Peifu controlled Hunan and Hupeh provinces, and Ichang, Changsha and Hankow. To the east, Sun Chuanfang – the Nanking warlord – controlled the lower Yangtze, as well as Kiangsi (Jiangsi), Anhwei (Anhui), Chekiang (Zhejiang), Fukien and Kiangsu (Jiangsu) provinces. On the upper Yangtze beyond the gorges, Yang Sen governed most of Szechuan (Sichuan) province. Chiang Kai-shek's 'Northern Offensive' began in the summer of 1926, and within six months the warlords Wu and Sun were in full retreat. As early as May 1925, anti-foreign riots had broken out in Shanghai,

Western gunboats pictured at their moorings off Hankow during the 1920s. USS *Monocacy* (the second Yangtze gunboat of that name) is in the foreground, while the USS *Isabel* lies behind her, accompanied by visiting American destroyers and a British sloop.

In 1922 the Japanese gunboat IJNS *Seta* was shipped to Shanghai in sections, and assembled there. She entered service the following year, based in Shanghai, and remained on the lower Yangtze for two decades, seeing action against the Chinese.

encouraged by the KMT. Foreign goods were boycotted and by June the rioting had spread to Hankow. Landing parties were sent ashore to protect the foreign concessions. Tensions were running high.

The situation wasn't helped by the Wanhsien Incident. In August 1926, troops loyal to the warlord Yang Sen tried to board the British-flagged SS *Wanliu*. In the process, a sampan overturned and Chinese soldiers were drowned. The *Wanliu* escaped, but two more British steamers were seized in Wanhsien: the *Wantung* and the *Wanhsien*. The local gunboat captain sent for help, and on 5 September the *Wantung* was stormed by a British boarding party. This recaptured the British crews, but seven British sailors and about 250 Chinese soldiers were killed in the fighting, while another 100 civilians were caught in the crossfire.

Propagandists claimed the Chinese death toll was anything up to 5,000, and that the British gunboats *Cockchafer* and *Widgeon* bombarded Wanhsien during the fight. These claims caused outrage and spawned anti-foreign rioting. The incident also coincided with the defeat of the independent warlord General Wu, which allowed the KMT to advance to the banks of the Yangtze. More Western sailors were landed to defend the *bund* (waterfront) at Hankow. A similarly tense situation developed at Changsha, where a British, an American and an Italian gunboat did what they could to help the foreign community there.

The steamer SS *Kiawo*, photographed leaving Hankow in 1926 with a naval boarding party on board, in response to the Wanhsien Incident. After steaming upriver, these sailors and marines attempted to recover two British-registered steamers held by a Chinese warlord.

In January 1927, the KMT entered Hankow. Westerners were evacuated to the gunboats and landing parties were reinforced. The next few days saw an orgy of bloodshed, as those who opposed the KMT were executed in the streets. The British finally handed over control of the British concession to the new Chinese authorities in an effort to diffuse the tension. It worked, Westerners soon began to return to the city. They were encouraged by naval reinforcements. By late January, 35 warships lay off Hankow – 11 British, 10 Japanese, nine American, three French and two Italian. Although they didn't intervene, their presence helped maintain calm.

The Insect Class gunboat HMS *Cockchafer*, pictured while patrolling the upper Yangtze during the early 1920s. She played a leading part in the Wanhsien Incident of 1926, when Lieutenant-Commander T. H. Whitehorn had to deal with the seizure of British-registered shipping.

Hankow was proclaimed the new nationalist capital, and KMT diplomats negotiated a deal with the Western powers, offering Chinese protection in return for a reduction in Western trading and legal privileges. The resulting Chen–O'Malley Agreement was duly signed, paving the way for Western recognition of the Nationalists. It was just as well, as fighting between the KMT and the warlords had resulted in a marked increase in banditry along the river, as disaffected soldiers of both sides formed roving bands.

In March 1927, the KMT occupied Nanking, and more anti-foreign rioting ensued. A group of Westerners working for Standard Oil were only rescued after the waiting Anglo-American flotilla laid down a barrage of protective fire. Rear-Admiral Henry Hough, commanding the Yangtze Patrol, oversaw the evacuation of the remaining foreigners, spurred by the threat of another bombardment. By then the political situation had altered again. Chiang Kai-shek's communist advisor Mikhail Borodin attempted a political coup, but failed to take control of the KMT. He fled into exile, but left behind letters proving he had been working for the Soviets. This prompted a split between the two political wings of the KMT, and the CCP broke away. From that point on the CCP followed its own political course.

This schism played out against the backdrop of increased tension in Shanghai, where communist-inspired strikes led to widespread unrest. The International Settlement there had recently been reinforced, and a military assault on the Westerners was thwarted. At that point, Chiang Kai-shek's moderates began a purge of communists, who abandoned their powerbase of Shanghai and fled into the countryside. Soon they and the nationalists

D   **USS *PANAY* OFF NANKING, 1937**

In July 1937, the Japanese invaded China, and the following month they landed an army at Shanghai. For the next five months, these troops forced back the Chinese nationalists, and advanced on Nanking, which was then the Chinese capital. The Western gunboats on the Yangtze did what they could to protect their nationals caught up in the fighting, but they were powerless to intervene in the conflict, or to prevent the suffering they witnessed all around them. On 11 December, the Chinese Army abandoned Nanking, and the USS *Panay* evacuated the last American civilians in the city. She then moved upstream a few miles, to protect three American oil tankers. At 8am the following morning, the *Panay* was still riding at anchor when she was attacked by 12 Japanese biplanes – a mixture of fighters and bombers – and she was hit by two small bombs. She sank shortly afterwards. Two of her crew were killed in the unprovoked attack, and dozens more were injured. The *Panay* Incident sparked a major diplomatic row, and hardened American public opinion against the 'warmongering' Japanese. This view of the incident shows the *Panay*'s crew trying vainly to defend themselves, as the Japanese planes attack their ship.

would be waging a bitter guerrilla war with each other. However, for the gunboat crews this situation, and the renewal of the nationalist advance northwards, meant that tensions gradually eased. Banditry remained a problem though, particularly on the upper Yangtze, and communist guerrilla bands roamed the lower river, but by 1928 Westerners for the most part were left in peace.

HMS *Scarab* lying off Nanking in late 1937, photographed during a Japanese bombing raid on the city. Unable to intervene, the Western powers could only watch as aircraft pounded the Chinese capital, which fell to the Imperial Japanese Army in December.

The River as a Battleground, 1931–41

In September 1931, the Japanese annexed Mongolia. By then Chiang Kai-shek had succeeded in uniting most of China, and only the communists and a few minor warlord bands remained. The struggle had drained the treasury, however, and the nationalists were unable to force the Japanese to withdraw. The Japanese took this as a sign of weakness. Anti-Japanese riots were countered by Japanese reinforcements in Shanghai and on the Yangtze.

In July 1937, the Japanese invaded northern China and occupied Peking (Beijing). In August, Japanese troops landed at Shanghai, while the Chinese built a boom across the Yangtze to prevent them from moving upriver towards Nanking. Thirteen British, six American and two French gunboats were now cut off from the open sea. In September, the Chinese abandoned Shanghai and the Japanese broke the boom. A second boom was built, however, midway between Chinkiang and Nanking. By October, Japanese aircraft were bombing Nanking every day, and all the gunboats painted national flags on their awnings, to reduce the risk of attack.

The Insect Class gunboat HMS *Ladybird*, pictured after she was shelled by Japanese shore batteries in December 1937 as she steamed past Wuhu. The Japanese later claimed they had no idea that British warships were operating on the Yangtze.

Rear-Admiral Reginald Holt, commanding the British Yangtze Flotilla, tried to negotiate a passage through the boom, as the Japanese captured Wuhu and encircled Nanking. On 11 December, Japanese guns began shelling HMS *Ladybird*, inflicting several hits before the ship pulled out of range. When HMS *Bee* arrived she too was shelled, before the Japanese could be convinced their targets were British rather than Chinese. Further up the river at Nanking, however, a great tragedy was unfolding.

The USS *Panay* was moored in the Yangtze, a few miles from Nanking, protecting a group of Standard Oil tankers. In the early afternoon of 12 December, she was attacked by 12 Japanese aircraft and was hit by two bombs. She sank soon afterwards, settling in shallow water. Two sailors were killed and many more injured, and it was not until the next day that the survivors were rescued, and taken downriver by an Anglo-American flotilla. Rear-Admiral Holt negotiated a safe passage through the boom, and the gunboats passed through the Japanese fleet without incident.

The *Panay* Incident caused outrage in the United States, and hardened American attitudes towards Japan. The international community was also horrified by the way the Japanese massacred their Chinese prisoners following the fall of Nanking on 13 December. During all this upheaval, though, relations between the Western gunboat crews and the Japanese Navy remained relatively cordial. The problem lay with the Japanese Army, not their fellow sailors.

After the *Panay*'s sinking in December 1937, her battered superstructure stood proud of the water, and her hulk remained there for several years. Some historians believe the attack on her may have been a deliberate act.

The sinking of the *Panay* took place almost exactly four years before the Japanese attack on Pearl Harbor. During the intervening years, the political climate on the Yangtze remained tense. The Japanese consolidated their hold on the lower Yangtze, and went on to capture Hankow. Trade of sorts resumed, but the Japanese were suspicious of Westerners, and often placed restrictions upon commerce and free navigation. Fuel remained precious, so gunboat movements were limited, and by mid-1938 most were used as station ships, guarding a particular port or installation, from Chungking to Shanghai.

In September 1939, Britain went to war with Germany, and many British gunboats sailed back to Europe. Others were decommissioned and their crews sent home. Businesses suffered too, as British and French authorities closed their Chinese offices and sent their staffs home. The Yangtze Flotilla was disbanded in 1940, and of the 13 gunboats present on the river in 1937, only four remained – two at Chungking, one at Changsha (both cities in Chinese hands) and one at Shanghai.

By late 1941, many of the American Yangtze Patrol vessels had also quit China. With much of the river under Japanese control, the American companies moved away, and by 1941 only a few stragglers remained in Shanghai. Three Yangtze Patrol gunboats set off across the South China Sea to join the Asiatic Fleet in Manila, leaving *Wake* (formerly *Guam*) at Shanghai and *Tutuila* on the upper Yangtze. Then, on 7 December 1941, the Japanese attacked Pearl Harbor. The United States and Great Britain were now at war with Japan. In Shanghai, the Japanese were well prepared, and overwhelmed the crew of the *Wake* before they could defend themselves. HMS *Peterel* offered a brief resistance before being sunk by the waiting Japanese warships.

HMS *Gannet* and her sister HMS *Peterel* were commissioned in 1927 as part of a modernization of the flotilla. *Gannet* was shipped to China in sections, and assembled in Shanghai. This photo of her was taken off Chungking in 1930.

The Yangtze Incident, 1949

For decades the Yangtze gunboats had been a regular sight on the great river, until world events overtook them. By the time Japan surrendered in August 1945, the gunboats' day had passed, and although the Western navies returned briefly to China, they no longer patrolled its inland

waters. By then the country was gripped by civil war, fought between the Chinese nationalists and communists. In 1949 the communists emerged victorious, and what remained of the nationalists fled to Taiwan, which became the Republic of China. On the mainland, Mao Tse-tung founded the People's Republic of China (PRC). Westerners were no longer welcome, an exclusion that lasted for almost half a century.

The Royal Navy sloop HMS *Amethyst* ran aground on the Yangtze in April 1949, after coming under heavy fire from Chinese communist shore batteries. After three months of diplomatic stalemate, she made a spectacular night-time escape downriver to safety.

Before this, though, there was one last gunboat-style action on the Yangtze. On 20 April 1949, the sloop HMS *Amethyst* made her way up the river from Shanghai to Nanking, with orders to protect the British consul there. She was fired on by communist shore batteries, and her wheelhouse was hit. *Amethyst* ran aground, and was then hit by over 50 more shells, and her captain mortally wounded. Her first lieutenant sent most of the men to safety on the nationalist side of the river, and two days later he refloated the *Amethyst*, anchoring out of range of the communist guns.

For the next ten weeks, *Amethyst* remained trapped 100 miles up the river. Negotiations proved fruitless, and so on the night of 30 July she slipped her anchor and ran down the river under cover of darkness. Having passed the gauntlet of batteries, she rammed and snapped a boom strung across the river to bar her escape. She finally reached safety, sending the signal 'Have rejoined the fleet off Woosung. God save the King.' Her dramatic exploit marked the end of a century of gunboat diplomacy on the Yangtze.

GUNBOAT DESIGN AND DEPLOYMENTS

The unique characteristics of the Yangtze meant that gunboats which served on its waters had to have certain characteristics. The spectacular seasonal fluctuation in water levels meant that they had to be of shallow draught, with screws and propeller shafts that were protected against accidental grounding. They needed to be small enough to be manoeuvrable, yet large enough to look impressive, and required relatively powerful engines to get them out of trouble quickly, and to force their way through the rapids of the Yangtze gorges to reach the upper river. The gunboats needed to be well-armed, or at least to give the appearance of being so, and had to be mechanically reliable, as they were often deployed hundreds of miles from the dockyard facilities of Shanghai.

Instead, what most Western navies were given were warships that weren't of much use anywhere else – the ageing cast-offs of larger fleets. It was only after World War I that purpose-built river gunboats began to appear on the Yangtze, and often they too were designed by people who had little idea of what service on the Yangtze was actually like. The following summary shows how the different naval powers struggled to find a gunboat design that was perfectly suited to this unique environment.

The Royal Navy

The first purpose-built British river gunboats to appear on the Yangtze were *Woodcock* and *Woodlark*, small vessels that were shipped to the Far East in sections and re-assembled in Shanghai. They were the first gunboats to reach the upper Yangtze, and their lack of armament and motive power was balanced by their shallow draught and their manoeuvrability. They were followed by a group of three more gunboats, which were essentially larger versions of the first two. *Teal*, *Moorhen* and *Widgeon* were still very primitive though, with only the most basic accommodation, no proper washing facilities and no electric power. Conditions improved, and by 1910 these gunboats were equipped with electric generators and wireless. Most were laid up during World War I, but when hostilities ended they were re-crewed, and a new influx of gunboats appeared to reinforce them.

All but one of the dozen gunboats of the Insect Class served on the Yangtze, although they had originally been designed for use on the Danube, where their heavy 6in guns were meant to overpower any Austro-Hungarian gunboats they encountered. They were equally impressive on the Yangtze, and for their size and primitive design they were singularly powerful warships that did their job well. During the early 1920s, HMS *Bee* became the flagship of the Rear-Admiral, Yangtze ('RAY'), and lost her main armament to provide more space for offices and accommodation.

The only real drawback with the class was that the vessels had a slightly deeper draught than earlier British gunboats, and so they could only make it through the gorges into the upper river during the summer months. Still, they had triple rudders, which made them very manoeuvrable, and from the early 1920s their steering gear was strengthened, which gave them an even tighter turning circle – a necessity in the gorges or to avoid collisions with poorly handled junks and sampans.

These powerful gunboats formed the mainstay of the Yangtze Flotilla until the late 1920s, when the decision was made to replace the remaining pre-Insect Class gunboats with modern vessels. The first of these were *Peterel* and *Gannet*, the first-named ship retaining her spelling mistake throughout her life. Both were large, high-sided vessels, purpose-built for service on the Yangtze. A third vessel, *Falcon*, was a smaller version of the first two, and entered service in 1931. Two similar but slightly smaller gunboats called *Tern* and *Seamew* – forerunners of the Peterel Class – were deployed on the West River, and were based in Hong Kong.

Unlike the Insect Class gunboats that followed her to China, HMS *Teal* was one of a kind, although like her predecessors she was shipped there in sections, and re-assembled in Shanghai. The design was later copied by the US Navy.

An Insect Class gunboat – probably HMS *Cicala* – moored off Hong Kong during the early 1920s. While most of the time these gunboats patrolled the Yangtze, they were occasionally called elsewhere, or sent to Hong Kong for repairs or a refit.

Two more gunboats arrived to join the flotilla before the outbreak of World War II in Europe. The small gunboat *Sandpiper* was built specifically to patrol the shallow waters of Tung Ting Lake and the Xiang River, and was based at Changsha. She assumed her duties in 1933, and four years later the gunboat *Scorpion* arrived to replace *Bee* as RAY flagship. Of course, gathering war clouds in Europe meant that the Royal Navy needed its men and ships in Europe, and by the time the last RAY, Rear-Admiral Holt, hauled down his flag in January 1940, many of these gunboats had already left the Yangtze, never to return.

The US Navy

The development of the Yangtze Patrol followed a similar course, although American parsimony meant that for decades the US Navy had to make do with gunboats that were barely up to the task. The first of these vessels, *Monocacy* and *Ashuelot*, were of American Civil War vintage – double-ended paddlewheelers whose paddle gearing had a tendency to jam at inopportune moments. Still, the two gunboats served out their days in Chinese waters.

From 1900 onwards an assortment of gunboats captured during the Spanish–American War (1898) began to appear on the Yangtze, and after the disposal of the *Monocacy* these constituted the sole American naval presence on the river for more than two decades. The largest of these gunboats was the *Elcano*, which usually served as the force flagship, based at Hankow. The *Quiros*, *Samar* and *Villalobos* were the other mainstays of the Yangtze Valley Force. The 'Spanish' gunboats were supported by the larger gunboat *Helena*, and occasionally by her sister-ship *Wilmington*. The British unkindly nicknamed *Helena* 'Jam Factory', on account of her overly tall funnel. This feature, however, seemed to impress the Chinese, and apart from the occasional visiting cruiser she was by far the largest warship on the river.

In 1914, this motley American force was joined by two new gunboats, *Monocacy* (the second Yangtze gunboat with the name) and her sister-ship *Palos*. These unpopular vessels were nicknamed 'Monotony' and 'Pathos' by their crews. Conditions on board were primitive, and they were awkward vessels to handle, being designed for use on the Great Lakes rather than the confined rivers of China.

Another of the new generation of British gunboats to reach the Yangtze during the 1920s was HMS *Sandpiper*, the smallest of the flotilla. This stylish vessel was designed for service around Changsha on the Xiang River, a tributary of the Yangtze.

Technically the stylish USS *Isabel* was a destroyer rather than a gunboat, although she was originally built as a private motor yacht. In 1921 she became the first flagship of the Yangtze Patrol, and remained on the river until 1928.

Still, they remained in service for a decade and a half, until their replacement by a force of custom-built river gunboats.

By the mid-1920s, it was clear that the gunboats of the newly designated Yangtze Patrol were rapidly approaching the end of their useful life. The US government made the decision to build six modern replacements, purpose-built for service on the Yangtze. These were built in Shanghai, and entered service in 1927. By that time *Quiros* and *Samar* had already been decommissioned, and *Wilmington* had returned home. That left *Monocacy*, *Palos*, *Villalobos*, *Elcano*, and *Helena*. The two remaining 'Spanish' gunboats were decommissioned in 1928, and *Helena* followed a year later. *Monocacy* lingered on the lower river until 1931,while *Palos* was finally decommissioned in 1937, after spending her last years as the Changsha guardship.

The 'new six' entered service in pairs. *Guam* was the first of them, commissioned in December 1927, and she proved a useful addition to the force. By the following year she was followed by her sister ship *Tutuila*, then the larger pair *Oahu* and *Panay*, which were 30ft longer and 80 tons heavier than the other two gunboats. This made them a little too large to negotiate the Yangtze gorges and reach the upper river. The final pair – *Luzon* and *Mindanao* – were larger still, 18ft longer and 120 tons heavier than the Panay Class gunboats. While they were powerful vessels, and looked splendid, their size made them even less suitable for service above Hankow than the previous vessels.

The gunboats of the Yangtze Patrol performed their job well, but after the sinking of the *Panay* in December 1937 they found themselves increasingly redundant, as American businesses abandoned the Yangtze basin when Japanese trade restrictions became too prohibitive. The countdown to Pearl Harbor had begun, and in the final weeks before the attack the majority of the American gunboats quit the Yangtze to join the Asiatic Fleet based in Manila. The loss of the *Guam* (renamed *Wake* in early 1941) and the handing over of *Tutuila* to the Chinese nationalists marked the end of active American involvement on the river.

The USS *Panay* was built in Shanghai, and entered service in 1927, one of a new generation of gunboats serving as part of the Yangtze Patrol. She was inadvertently attacked and sunk by Japanese aircraft off Nanking in December 1937.

HMS *CICALA*, INSECT CLASS GUNBOAT, *c.* 1927

The Insect Class of gunboats were unique in the Royal Navy, as they were originally built for service on the Danube, designed to outgun and outfight their Austro-Hungarian counterparts. In the end they spent World War I and its immediate aftermath fighting on the rivers of Mesopotamia (now Iraq) and in northern Russia. The majority of them were then sent to the Far East, where they served on the Yangtze. Like her dozen sister ships, HMS *Cicala* may have been named after an insect, but she carried a powerful sting – she was armed with two 6in guns. These gunboats performed sterling service in China, and remained there until the start of World War II. HMS *Cicala* was sunk by Japanese dive-bombers on 21 December 1941, while attempting to defend Hong Kong.

Specifications

Displacement: 645 tons

Dimensions: Length: 237ft 6in; Beam: 36ft; Draught: 4ft

Propulsion: Two Yarrow engines and boilers, producing 2,000 steam horsepower

Maximum speed: 14 knots

Armament: Two single 6in guns; one 12-pounder (3in) anti-aircraft gun; later replaced by a single 2-pounder Pom-Pom; six single .303in Maxim machine-guns

Armour: 5/8in plate armour on gunshields and superstructure (proof against small-arms fire); gunshields and bridge reinforced by 1in steel plate in 1928

Complement: 55 officers and men

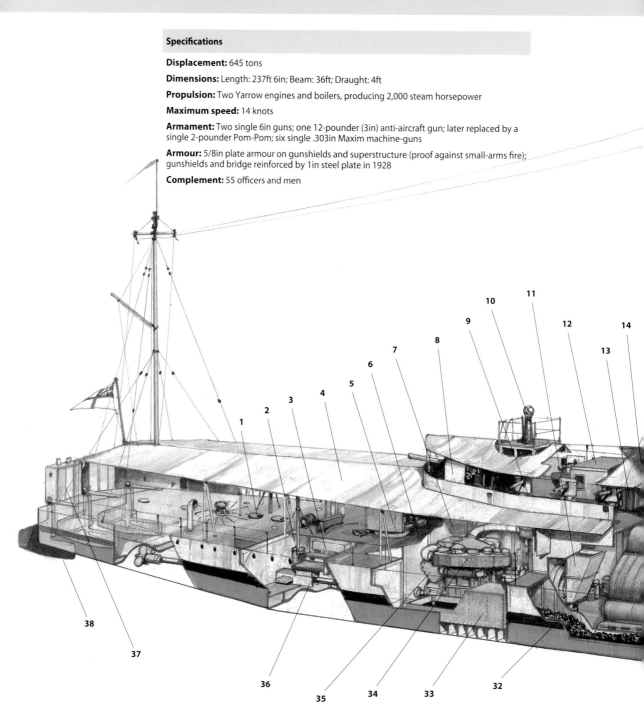

Key

1. Scuttles
2. Stove
3. Crew space
4. Awnings
5. 6in gun
6. Aft magazine
7. Engine room
8. 12-pounder (3") AA gun
9. .303in machine-guns
10. Compass platform
11. 72in fan and intake (2)
12. Fresh water tanks
13. WT. office
14. Boiler (2)
15. Bridge
16. 2-pounder Pom-Pom
17. 6in gun
18. Ward room
19. Commander's quarters
20. Surgeon's quarters
21. Sub-Lieutenant's quarters
22. Awning supports
23. Crew space
24. Capstan
25. Naval stores
26. Keel
27. Gun support
28. Oil fuel tanks
29. Forward magazine
30. Fresh water tank
31. Oil fuel tank
32. Coal bunker
33. Oil fuel tank
34. Engine (2)
35. Condenser
36. Shaft casing
37. Seamen's heads (W.C.)
38. Rudder

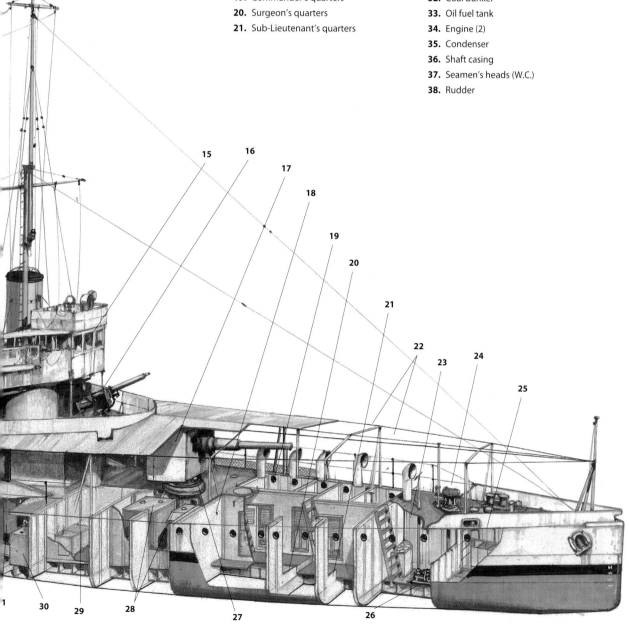

The Imperial Japanese Navy

The Japanese were relative latecomers to the Yangtze, arriving after their victory in the Russo–Japanese War. Their first trio of Yangtze gunboats – *Uji*, *Fushimi* and *Sumida* – were all built in Britain, and while the *Uji* was not a proper river gunboat, the others were shallow-drafted and ideal for service on the river. The *Fushimi* was even small and powerful enough to pass through the Yangtze gorges and patrol the upper river. Two more gunboats – the *Toba* and the *Saga* – arrived at the start of World War I, and while the *Toba* remained on the Yangtze until 1944, the *Saga* was moved to the West River during the late 1920s. By that time the force had been augmented by four Seta Class gunboats – *Seta*, *Katada*, *Honzu* and *Hira*, which formed the 11th Gunboat Sentai (Flotilla). In addition, the large and powerful *Ataka* served as the flotilla flagship, although her 950-ton displacement made her unsuitable for operations above the lower river.

By 1930, this large Japanese force was augmented by the two Atami Class gunboats – *Futami* and *Atami* – which had sufficiently shallow draught to operate on Tung Ting Lake and the Xiang River. Finally the small gunboat *Sumida* served on the upper and middle Yangtze from 1931. During the Sino–Japanese War, Japanese fleet destroyers and even light cruisers operated in support of the Imperial Japanese Army as it advanced upriver from Shanghai to Hankow, and during World War II they were boosted by a number of other gunboats, either newly built in Japan or captured from the Allies. Yet by August 1945 many of these gunboats had been sunk or damaged, and those that remained were either scrapped by the Allies, or handed over to the Chinese nationalists.

The Imperial German Navy

The Germans established themselves in China in 1897, but they had relatively little to do with the Yangtze, as their main sphere of interest was around Tsingtao and Shantung province, on the Yellow Sea. However, the pair of large seagoing gunboats *Tiger* and *Luchs* ventured upriver as far as Hankow, while another pair, *Iltis* and *Jaguar*, patrolled the lower Yangtze and Xi (West) River respectively. The only German gunboats to remain on the Yangtze throughout the year were the converted Yangtze steamer *Vorwärts* and the purpose-built *Vaterland*, which was shipped to Shanghai in sections and then rebuilt. Her sister ship the *Tsingtao* also operated on the Xi River.

Vorwärts was decommissioned in 1909, and replaced by the nimble 314-ton gunboat *Otter*, which was built in Shanghai. Tsingtao also served as the base for the German Asiatic Squadron, but apart from making visits to Shanghai, the squadron played no part in the patrolling of the Chinese rivers. In the summer of 1914, the German gunboats that still remained on the Yangtze were either interned, decommissioned or scuttled.

The French Navy

Although seagoing French gunboats had patrolled the Chinese waterways from 1860 onwards, it was 1900 before a

The IJNS *Ataka* was another well-known sight on the Yangtze, serving as the Japanese flagship. This picture of her was taken in the mid-1920s – in 1937 she returned to Japan where she was modernized, before being sent to Singapore.

permanent French flotilla was established, with the arrival of the two Argus Class river gunboats – *Argus* and *Vigilante*. They were built in Britain by Thornycroft, which also designed the British Woodlark Class. Consequently, the two classes were very similar. They were re-assembled in Hong Kong, and spent the next 14 years patrolling the Xi River. The following year, the *Olry* arrived in Shanghai and was sent up the Yangtze to Hankow. That December she reached Chungking on the upper river, and remained there until 1909, when a boiler accident forced her to return to Shanghai. The damage was eventually deemed too extensive to repair, and she was decommissioned. The tiny *Ta Kiang* also served on the upper river from 1901 to 1904, until she too was sold.

The French lacked a permanent presence on the lower Yangtze until 1922, when two purpose-built gunboats of the Doudart de Lagrée Class were shipped to the Orient, and re-assembled in Shanghai. *Doudart de Lagrée* and *Balny* served on the Yangtze until the start of World War II. They were one of two inter-war reinforcements, the other being the smaller Vigilante Class gunboats *Argus* and *Vigilante* – the second pair of French gunboats with those names. They spent the bulk of their service life on the Xi River, or on French Indochina's Red River, and both gunboats were decommissioned in 1940.

Finally, in the late 1920s two even more impressive French gunboats arrived on the Yangtze. From 1922 the sloop *Alerte* was based at Hankow, and patrolled the Yangtze as far as Ichang, until she was recalled to France in 1936. The even more impressive *Francis Garnier* arrived in 1927, and with a displacement of 640 tons she was the largest French gunboat on the river and the flagship of the French flotilla. When World War II began she was sent to Indochina, where she was eventually scuttled.

The Regia Marina

The Italians had very limited financial interests in the Yangtze basin, but between the world wars they maintained a token presence on the river, and in the treaty ports. The elegant gunboat *Sebastiano Caboto* appeared on the river in 1920, but her deep draught made her a seasonal visitor rather than a Yangtze regular. She returned to Italy shortly before World War II began. Similarly the *Ermanno Carlotto* and the *Lepanto* (which joined her in 1927), although shallow-draughted, were normally based in Tientsin, but took turns to patrol the Yangtze as far as Ichang. These two Italian gunboats were moved to Shanghai in 1938, and remained there until Italy's surrender in 1943, when they were scuttled. They were subsequently raised by the Japanese, and after the war they were handed over to the Chinese nationalists.

The French Navy maintained a small squadron of gunboats on the Yangtze, and also on the Xi River. The 200-ton *Argus*, built in 1922, was one of two Vigilante Class gunboats, and served on the Xi until 1940.

LIFE ON THE GUNBOATS

The elegant *Sebastiano Cabato* was the first of two Italian gunboats to patrol the Yangtze after World War I, although she also served at Shanghai and Tientsin. She remained in Chinese waters until 1934, when she returned to Italy.

The crews of the Yangtze gunboats had a strange existence. Their vessels frequently lacked the most basic comforts, but they were popular with the foreign sailors who served in them, as Chinese crewmen often performed the more menial duties such as washing clothes, scrubbing decks and cooking meals. Most gunboats had a crew of about two dozen – two or three officers, about six petty officers or leading hands, and around 16–20 ordinary seamen. These were supported by a Chinese crew of about six official members and as many unofficial ones, whose number included a chief steward ('Number One Boy'), a cook and several stewards, laundrymen and deckhands.

The captain of a gunboat had his own substantial living quarters, while the officers shared a wardroom and the senior rates had their own mess. The rest of the Western crew tended to share a mess deck (crew quarters), albeit a reasonably commodious one, while the Chinese crew berthed below the waterline, in the tiller flat. The Chinese were considered additional staff, and no Western gunboat was designed or constructed with accommodation or living quarters for them. These ships were operated on a strictly hierarchical basis. Life for the officers was reasonably comfortable, and duties were often minimal. An American officer described the accommodation on board the USS *Elcano*:

> The Captain's Quarters were fairly commodious for such a small ship. They were aft, and because of the hull conformation, shaped like the end of a bath tub. The skipper enjoyed the luxury of a tub and flush toilet, but lesser officers used a small steel cubicle on deck, barely large enough to squeeze into, which housed shower and archaic sanitary facilities. Just forward of the captain's cabin was wardroom country, with two small staterooms on each side of the ship, opening directly into the very small rectangular wardroom itself.

With the exception of HMS *Falcon*, British gunboats had the same poor sanitary arrangements – box-like structures overhanging the stern were provided, and the combined heads and showers remained a distinctive feature of British river gunboats throughout the period. Once, when a female guest

 SEBASTIANO CABOTO (ITALIAN, 1925); IJNS HONZU (JAPANESE, 1934)

While the British, Americans, Japanese and French operated the largest gunboat flotillas on the Yangtze, other nations also kept a small presence there. The Italian gunboat *Sebastiano Caboto* (above) was built in 1913 and was sent to Tientsin, where the Italians maintained a minor naval force. During the 1920s, these gunboats toured the Chinese treaty ports, and sailed up the Yangtze as far as Hankow. *Sebastiano Caboto* was far too deep-draughted to be an effective river gunboat, and she soon returned downriver. In 1926 she was sent to Shanghai, to protect Italian interests there, but after that, apart from regular visits to Shanghai and Hankow, she was based in Tientsin, until her return to Italy in 1935.

By contrast the IJNS *Honzu* (below) – a Japanese Seta Class gunboat – was one of several similar vessels that entered service during the 1920s, designed specifically to patrol the great rivers of China. The *Honzu* formed part of the 11th Gunboat Sentai (Flotilla), based in Shanghai, where by 1925 the Japanese had become the largest foreign element in the International Settlement. She also patrolled the Yangtze, and was still there at the outbreak of the Sino–Japanese War in 1937, when she operated in support of the Imperial Japanese Army.

asked their purpose, an officer discreetly replied, 'That, Madam, is where we deal with our secret papers!'

The wardroom on an Insect Class gunboat was a little more civilized. On British gunboats officers' quarters were forward, and those of the men further aft, a reversal of the traditional arrangement. The wardroom has been described as a miniature version of a London gentlemen's club, with comfortable armchairs draped in white cloth, copies of *The Times* (usually several weeks old) and white-coated Chinese stewards, ready to serve a pink gin when required. In port the officers spent a lot of time ashore, either on shooting parties or playing tennis at a fashionable Hankow or Shanghai club. On American ships, one officer was required to remain on board at all times. The inevitable quip quoted by one American officer on the Yangtze was that 'when Greek meets Greek they start a restaurant. When two US naval officers get together they start a watch list, and when two British naval officers meet they start a tennis club'.

For the ship's company – the men the US Navy called 'River Rats' – pleasures were less rarefied. In British ships a daily tot of rum was served, while the French, Italians and Germans served wine to the crew. American ships were dry, so one of the main aims of the crew was to blow what money they had in a 'run ashore' in Hankow or – better still – Shanghai. Shanghai was the ultimate place to unwind. Bars and brothels were plentiful, and with warships of so many nationalities in port the scope for bar brawls was extensive. Other ports were less inviting. Lieutenant Douglas Claris, a British officer, said of Ichang in 1911 that while there was a small recreational club where officers were welcomed, all the men had to enjoy was 'a naval canteen for the bluejackets'. He recommended that as it was so poorly stocked, gunboats visiting from Ichang should bring their own beer.

American sailors were usually better paid than their British equivalents, but while on patrol had little to spend their money on. As one officer put it: 'After a long dark, rainy winter and with everything ashore knee-deep in mud, every man had squirreled away the equivalent of a half-bucket or more of silver dollars, burning to be invested in some way or other.' Concerning such investment, a River Rat explained his philosophy: 'The most of it goes for likker and wimmen [*sic*]. The rest I spend foolishly.'

The multinational aspect of naval life on the Yangtze meant that a lot of time and effort was spent on ceremonial duties, courtesy visits, keeping ships spotless in the presence of foreign navies and generally indulging in pomp and ceremony. Fortunately, Chinese rivermen and their families

The USS *Elcano* was one of several old gunboats captured from the Spanish during the Spanish–American War (1898). She carried four 4in guns, one of which is seen here during a firing exercise. She remained in service from 1902 until 1928.

usually offered to keep the hull sides spotless in exchange for food waste and scraps. The Chinese crew looked after everything else, polishing, painting and scrubbing the gunboats until they looked their best, however worn and antiquated they might be.

The monotony of river life was broken by occasional moments of danger. For the most part, this involved going into action against pirates. Whatever the nationality of the gunboat crew, their main brief was to protect their fellow countrymen while they lived and worked in China. Most of these Western civilians were either in China on business, working as missionaries or on board merchant vessels operating on the Yangtze. The gunboats' roles, therefore, could involve escorting merchant steamers past known bandit hotspots, rescuing vessels that had been taken over by pirates posing as passengers, or – occasionally – setting ashore an armed landing party to protect Western businesses or homes from rioters.

In theory, the discretionary powers given to naval officers meant that gunboats were perfectly entitled to fire on a Chinese port or for a landing party to shoot into a Chinese mob without any major concerns about diplomatic niceties. The policy of 'extraterritoriality' also meant that for the most part Westerners were not beholden to Chinese law, and effectively benefited from diplomatic immunity in China. This meant that the commanders of these little gunboats, and the naval commander-in-chief in the region, had all the diplomatic and naval tools they needed to protect their country's national interests. Of course, this could also turn an ugly situation into a full-scale crisis.

Such is exactly what happened during the Wanhsien Incident of 1926, when two British-registered steamers were seized by troops belonging to a local Chinese warlord. A British boarding party succeeded in freeing the British crewmen, but in the process a full-scale firefight developed, which involved the gunboats

During the first three decades of the 20th century, Shanghai was a bustling international port and the gateway to the Yangtze River. Gunboat and warship crews of all nationalities saw Shanghai as an extremely lively place for a 'run ashore'.

American sailors stand on the edge of the *bund* at Hankow, while in the background the USS *Monocacy* is berthed alongside a floating pontoon. The fluctuating levels of the river made it impossible to tie up alongside a conventional quayside.

35

Widgeon and *Cockchafer* firing at Chinese troops. According to the official British estimate, the Royal Navy destroyed 20 houses and killed up to 100 civilians, as well as about 250 soldiers. These sorts of actions only served to inflame tensions between the Chinese and the 'foreigners'.

During the clash between Chiang Kai-shek's nationalists and the Chinese warlords in 1926, landing parties were sent ashore in Hankow, Nanking and Shanghai to help protect Western interests. Sandbagged machine-gun emplacements were created and barbed-wire barricades were used to protect the Western quarters. In January 1927, a full-scale riot developed in Hankow, as a pro-nationalist mob threatened to overrun the foreign district. In the end, though, apart from a few injuries from hurled stones, no real crisis developed, as the British and Americans drew bayonets but didn't fire into the crowd. The situation was also calmed by the arrival of naval reinforcements – an international flotilla of seagoing warships.

The rioting in Shanghai and Nanking was far more extensive. At one point, the US warships *Noa* and *Preston* and the British cruiser *Emerald* fired their main guns in an attempt to protect Western fugitives from rampaging nationalist troops. An American ensign amongst the fugitive party directed the fire using signal flags. He later recalled: 'It wasn't three minutes after our first signal to commence firing that the first salvo landed. The gunfire was most effective, and undoubtedly saved all our lives...The soldiers ran like frightened rabbits, but not until we had killed three or four of them ourselves.'

Actions of this kind were rare – the more typical engagement involved coming under fire from bandits or rogue soldiers on the shore, and firing back. For instance, in 1930 USS *Palos* and HMS *Teal* had come under fire from communist guerrillas during riots in Changsha. A crewman on board *Palos* later described the action: 'Both 3-inch guns were swung into action, and the *Palos* became a death-dealing piece of machinery...Every man on the ship was doing his part, every man had a certain duty to perform, many were fighting with little or no protection from the Communist gunfire.' *Palos* subdued the guerrillas, but afterwards more than 100 bullet holes were counted in her hull, superstructure and funnel. Fortunately, Chinese accuracy during this period was notoriously deficient, as the soldiers, bandits or guerrillas who shot at the gunboats were usually extremely poorly trained.

The sometimes monotonous, sometimes lively and invariably unusual existence of the Yangtze River Rat lasted from 1900 when the first real gunboats arrived on the river, and continued until 1937, when the Yangtze

G **THE LAST OF THE GUNBOATS: USS *GUAM* (1932); HMS *PETEREL* (1937)**

One of the six modern gunboats to enter service with the Yangtze Patrol, the USS *Guam* (above) had an unusual career. Like her sister ship USS *Tutuila*, she entered service in 1927, at a time when the political tensions caused by the advance of the KMT had abated. She spent the next decade dealing with bandits, communist insurgents and river pirates, but after the sinking of the USS *Panay* in 1937 she was based in Shanghai and on the lower Yangtze, where she monitored Japanese naval movements. She was renamed USS *Wake* in early 1941, and that December she was captured by the Japanese, before her crew even realized that they were at war.

Like the *Guam*, HMS *Peterel* (below) was built in 1927 – her unusual name was the result of a clerical spelling mistake in the Admiralty. Also like the *Guam*, she spent the next decade based at Hankow on the Yangtze, but in December 1941 she was lying off Shanghai, the last British gunboat on the river. Unlike the *Guam* she refused to surrender, and was sunk by gunfire from the powerful Japanese flotilla based in the harbour. She became the first British warship to be sunk by the Japanese in the war.

became a theatre of war. The Sino–Japanese War then effectively acted as a precursor for the larger global conflict that followed. The River Rats and their gunboats drifted away, to serve elsewhere, and a colourful era in naval social history came to an end. Today they have passed into history. One old 'River Rat' – a survivor of the *Panay* Incident – recalled that the Yangtze Patrol reunions were well attended, and old sailors arrived by the busload. Just before he died in 2009 he reckoned he was one of the last of them – a sailor from a long-forgotten era.

BRITISH AND AMERICAN GUNBOATS

The following list covers the major Royal Navy and US Navy gunboats operating in Chinese coastal and riverine waters from 1900 until 1941. Space precludes a similar treatment of Japanese and French gunboats, or those of the lesser maritime powers who operated in Chinese waters during this period. However, the excellent website www.HMSFalcon.com contains a list of most of these, as does Haines (1973), listed in the bibliography.

British Gunboats – The Yangtze Flotilla

Woodcock Class	
Gunboats in class	2 – *Woodcock, Woodlark*
Displacement	150 tons
Dimensions	Length: 148ft; Beam: 24ft; Draught: 2ft
Power	550 steam horsepower
Speed	13 knots
Armament	Two single 6-pounders, four single machine-guns
Complement	25 officers and men

Woodcock: Commissioned 1897, decommissioned 1928. Served principally on the upper Yangtze.
Woodlark: Commissioned 1897, decommissioned 1928. Served principally on the upper Yangtze.

Heron Class

Gunboats in class	4 – *Nightingale, Robin, Sandpiper, Snipe*
Displacement	85 tons
Dimensions	Length: 108ft; Beam: 20ft; Draught: 2ft
Power	240 steam horsepower
Speed	9 knots
Armament	Two single 6-pounders, four single machine-guns
Complement	25 officers and men

Nightingale: Commissioned 1897, decommissioned 1919. Served principally on the middle Yangtze.

Robin: Commissioned 1897, decommissioned 1928. Served principally on the Xi River

Sandpiper: Commissioned 1898, decommissioned 1920. Served principally on the Xi River

Snipe: Commissioned 1898, decommissioned 1919. Served principally on the middle Yangtze.

Moorhen Class

Gunboats in class	2 – *Moorhen, Teal*
Displacement	85 tons
Dimensions	Length: 165ft; Beam: 24ft 6in; Draught: 2ft
Power	670 steam horsepower
Speed	13 knots
Armament	Two single 6-pounders, four single machine-guns
Complement	35 officers and men

Teal: Commissioned 1901, decommissioned 1931. Served principally on the middle and upper Yangtze. Paid off 1914–18, and re-commissioned in 1919.

Moorhen: Commissioned 1901, decommissioned 1933. Served principally on the middle and upper Yangtze. Paid off 1914–18, and re-commissioned in 1919.

In May 1900, HMS *Woodcock* (pictured here) and her sister ship HMS *Woodlark* were the first Western gunboats to navigate the Yangtze gorges and reach the upper Yangtze. They remained on station there for more than a quarter of a century.

Widgeon Class

Gunboats in class	1 – *Widgeon*
Displacement	195 tons
Dimensions	Length: 165ft; Beam: 24ft 6in; Draught: 2ft
Power	670 steam horsepower
Speed	13 knots
Armament	Two single 6-pounders, four single machine-guns
Complement	35 officers and men

Near-sister of the Moorhen Class gunboats.

Widgeon: Commissioned 1904, decommissioned 1931. Served principally on the middle and upper Yangtze. Paid off 1914–18, and re-commissioned in 1919.

Kinsha Class

Gunboats in class	1 – *Kinsha*
Displacement	616 tons
Dimensions	Length: 192ft; Beam: 20ft; Draught: 7ft
Power	1,200 steam horsepower
Speed	14 knots
Armament	Two single 12-pounders, seven single machine-guns
Complement	58 officers and men

Kinsha: A river steamer, purchased into service. Commissioned 1900, decommissioned 1921. Served principally on the lower and middle Yangtze. Paid off 1914–18, and briefly re-commissioned in 1919, when she served as the Yangtze Flotilla flagship (1920–21).

Insect Class

Gunboats in class	12 – *Aphis, Bee, Cicala, Cricket, Cockchafer, Glowworm, Gnat, Ladybird, Mantis, Moth, Scarab, Tarantula*
Displacement	645 tons
Dimensions	Length: 237ft 6in; Beam: 36ft; Draught: 4ft
Power	2,000 steam horsepower
Speed	14 knots

HMS *Aphis* in Chinkiang in 1937, when she was trapped in the Yangtze by Chinese blockships and sunk to prevent the Japanese from reaching Nanking. Union Jacks were painted on her awnings to deter Japanese aircraft from attacking her by mistake.

Armament	Two single 6in/40 QF ('Quick-Firing') guns (Mark I), two 12-pounder (3in) QF guns, six single machine-guns. This armament varied over time, but in the Yangtze Flotilla most Insect Class gunboats had their after 12-pounder replaced by a single 2-pounder Pom-Pom.
Complement	53 officers and men

Aphis: Commissioned 1915, decommissioned and broken up in 1947. Before being sent to the China Station, she served in Mesopotamia (1915–18) – now Iraq – and on the Danube (1918–22). Temporarily decommissioned in Malta 1922–27, before being sent to Shanghai. Served principally on the Yangtze (1927–40). In 1940 she was sent to the Mediterranean.

Bee: Commissioned 1915, decommissioned March 1939. Before being sent to the China Station she served in Mesopotamia (1915–17). Served principally on the Yangtze (1918–39). In 1927 she became the flagship of the Yangtze Flotilla.

Cicala: Commissioned 1915, sunk in Hong Kong, 21 December 1941. Saw service in World War I in home waters and in northern Russia, before being sent to the China Station in 1920. Served principally on the Xi River (1920–41).

Cricket: Commissioned 1915, damaged by bombing off Tobruk 29 June 1941, taken to Port Said and beached. Decommissioned in 1942. Saw service in World War I in home waters and in northern Russia, before being sent to the China Station in 1920. Served principally on the Yangtze (1920–40). In November 1940 she was sent to the Mediterranean.

Cockchafer: Commissioned 1915, decommissioned 1947. Broken up in 1949. Saw service in World War I in home waters and in northern Russia, before being sent to the Far East in 1920. Served principally on the Yangtze (1920–40). In March 1940 she was sent to the Persian Gulf.

Glowworm: Commissioned 1915, decommissioned 1922, sold 1928. Saw service in World War I in home waters and in northern Russia, before being decommissioned in Malta. She was the only Insect Class gunboat that never served on the China Station.

Gnat: Commissioned 1915, torpedoed off Malta 21 October 1941, and decommissioned. Broken up in 1945. Before being sent to the China Station, she served in Mesopotamia (1915–17). Served principally on the Yangtze (1918–40). In 1940 she was sent to the Mediterranean.

Ladybird: Commissioned 1916, sunk off Tobruk 12 May 1941. Before being sent to the China Station she served in Mesopotamia (1915–18), and on the Danube (1918–22). Temporarily decommissioned in Malta 1922–27, before being sent to Shanghai. Served principally on the Yangtze (1927–40). In 1940 she was sent to the Mediterranean. After her sinking in shallow water, her decks remained above water, and she was used as a static anti-aircraft battery until 1942.

Mantis: Commissioned 1916, decommissioned January 1940. Before being sent to the China Station she served in Mesopotamia (1915–18). Served principally on the Yangtze (1920–40).

Moth: Commissioned 1916, scuttled in Hong Kong 21 December 1941. Before being sent to the China Station she served in Mesopotamia (1915–18). Served principally on the Xi River (1920–37). After her sinking she was raised by the Japanese, refitted and renamed the IJNS *Suma*. She was mined and sunk on the Yangtze on 19 March 1945.

Scarab: Commissioned 1916, decommissioned 1947. Broken up in 1948. Before being sent to the China Station she served in Mesopotamia (1915–18). Served principally on the Yangtze (1918–41). In late 1941 she was sent to the Mediterranean.

Tarantula: Commissioned 1916, decommissioned 1946 and sunk as a target off Ceylon. Before being sent to the China Station she served in Mesopotamia (1915–18). Served principally on the Xi River (1918–37).

Tern Class

Gunboats in class	2 – *Tern, Seamew*
Displacement	262 tons
Dimensions	Length: 168ft; Beam: 27ft; Draught: 5ft
Power	1,370 steam horsepower
Speed	14 knots
Armament	Two single 3in HA ('High-Angle') anti-aircraft guns, eight single machine-guns
Complement	55 officers and men

Tern: Commissioned 1927, scuttled off Hong Kong 19 December 1941. Served principally on the Xi River (1928–41).

Seamew: Commissioned 1928, decommissioned 1947 and scrapped. Served principally on the Xi River (1928–41).

Peterel Class

Gunboats in class	2 – Peterel, Gannet
Displacement	310 tons
Dimensions	Length: 185ft; Beam: 29ft; Draught: 4ft
Power	2,250 steam horsepower
Speed	16 knots
Armament	Two single 3in HA anti-aircraft guns, eight single machine-guns
Complement	55 officers and men

An improved version of the Tern Class.

Peterel: Commissioned 1927, sunk by gunfire off Shanghai, 7 December 1941. Served principally on the Yangtze (1927–39) and as Shanghai guardship (1939–41).

Gannet: Commissioned 1928, decommissioned 1940 at Chungking. Served principally on the Xi River (1928–40). In 1942 she was handed over to the Chinese Navy.

Falcon Class

Gunboats in class	1 – Falcon
Displacement	372 tons
Dimensions	Length: 150ft; Beam: 28ft 9in; Draught: 6ft
Power	2,250 steam horsepower
Speed	15 knots
Armament	One single 3.7in howitzer, two 6-pounder guns, eight single machine-guns
Complement	55 officers and men

Falcon: Commissioned 1932, decommissioned March 1941 at Chungking. Served principally on the Yangtze (1932–41). In 1942 she was handed over to the Chinese Navy.

In 1920 the Insect Class gunboat HMS *Bee* had her main armament removed to make room for extra cabins, part of her conversion into a headquarters ship – the flagship of the Rear-Admiral, Yangtze (RAY), who was usually based at Hankow.

Sandpiper Class

Gunboats in class	1 – *Sandpiper*
Displacement	185 tons
Dimensions	Length: 167ft 3in; Beam: 30ft 9in; Draught: 2ft
Power	600 steam horsepower
Speed	11 knots
Armament	One single 3.7in howitzer, one single 6-pounder gun, 4 single machine-guns
Complement	35 officers and men

Sandpiper: Commissioned 1933, decommissioned March 1941 at Changsha. Served principally on the Xiang River, as the Changsha guardship (1933–41). In 1942 she was handed over to the Chinese Navy.

US Gunboats – The Yangtze Patrol

Monocacy Class

Gunboats in class	2 – *Monocacy* (I), *Ashuelot*
Displacement	1,370 tons
Dimensions	Length: 265ft; Beam: 35ft; Draught: 9ft
Power	800 steam horsepower (sidewheel steamer)
Speed	11 knots
Armament	Four 8in muzzle-loading smoothbores, two 60-pounder muzzle-loading rifles
Complement	159 officers and men

Monocacy: Commissioned 1866, decommissioned 1903. Served throughout the Asiatic Station (1871–1901), but until 1899 she made frequent patrols up the Yangtze. She last saw action in 1900–01, during the Boxer Uprising. Although technically *Monocacy* had ceased to serve on the Yangtze by 1900, she is worth listing here as she was still on station in that year, and because she was the first of two warships of the same name to operate on the Yangtze.

Ashuelot: Commissioned 1866, wrecked and sunk off Amoy 1883.

The 'Spanish' Gunboats

As noted previously, during the Spanish–American War several Spanish gunboats were captured, and many were pressed into service with the US Navy. Some were sent to China, where they served on the Yangtze.

Elcano (PG-38)

Displacement	620 tons
Dimensions	Length: 156ft; Beam: 23ft; Draught: 7ft 6in
Power	660 steam horsepower
Speed	11 knots
Armament	Four 4in guns
Complement	103 officers and men

Launched in Cadiz, Spain, 1885. Captured in Manila Bay, 1898. Commissioned 1902, decommissioned and sunk as target 1928. Principally served on the Yangtze (1902–27).

Quiros (PG-40)

Displacement	350 tons
Dimensions	Length: 145ft; Beam: 22ft 9in; Draught: 7ft 9in
Power	450 steam horsepower
Speed	11 knots
Armament	Four 6-pounder guns, two 3-pounder guns
Complement	57 officers and men

Launched in Hong Kong, 1895. Commissioned 1900. Captured in Manila Bay, 1898. Decommissioned and sunk as target 1923. Principally served on the Yangtze (1905–23).

Samar (PG-41)

Displacement	243 tons
Dimensions	Length: 121ft; Beam: 18ft; Draught: 7ft 6in
Power	250 steam horsepower
Speed	10½ knots
Armament	One 6-pounder gun, one 3-pounder gun, two 1-pounder guns
Complement	28 officers and men

Captured in Manila Bay, 1898. Commissioned 1899, decommissioned 1921. Principally served on the Yangtze (1900–19).

Villalobos (PG-42)

Displacement	270 tons
Dimensions	Length: 156ft; Beam: 23ft; Draught: 7ft 6in6in
Power	450 steam horsepower
Speed	11 knots
Armament	Four 3-pounder guns, two 1-pounder guns
Complement	57 officers and men

Launched in Hong Kong, 1895. Commissioned 1900. Captured in Manila Bay, 1898. Decommissioned and sunk as target 1928. Principally served on the Yangtze (1901–28). Incidentally, the Villalobos was used as the model for the San Pablo, the fictional gunboat portrayed in The Sand Pebbles.

The Shanghai-built gunboat USS *Tutuila* joined the Yangtze Patrol in 1928, and she remained on the river until December 1941, when she was withdrawn to the Philippines. She is pictured here off Chunking in 1937, during a Japanese bombing raid.

Wilmington Class

Gunboats in class	2 – Wilmington, Helena
Displacement	1,397 tons
Dimensions	Length: 250ft 9in; Beam: 40ft; Draught: 9ft
Power	1,890 steam horsepower
Speed	15 knots
Armament	Eight 4in RF guns, four 6-pounder guns, four 1-pounder guns, four machine-guns
Complement	175 officers and men

Wilmington (PG-8): Launched in Newport News, VA, 1895. Commissioned 1897, decommissioned 1946. Participated in the Spanish–American War (1898), before she saw service in Chinese waters (1901–04), primarily showing the flag in coastal treaty ports. She subsequently served on the Yangtze (1900–12), before returning to general service with the Asiatic Fleet. From 1919 to 1922 she served on the Yangtze again, before returning to home waters in late 1922. She ended her active life as a training vessel. Renamed *Dover* (1941), and reclassified as IX-30.

Helena (PG-9): Launched in 1896. Commissioned 1897, decommissioned 1932. Participated in the Spanish–American War (1898), before she saw service in Chinese waters (1900–29), primarily serving on the Yangtze. In 1929 she joined the South China Patrol, until her decommissioning three years later.

Monocacy Class

Gunboats in class	2 – Monocacy (II), Palos
Displacement	190 tons
Dimensions	Length: 165ft 6in; Beam: 24ft 6in; Draught: 2ft 6in
Power	800 steam horsepower
Speed	13½ knots
Armament	Two 6-pounder guns, six single machine-guns
Complement	47 officers and men

Monocacy (PG-15): Launched in Shanghai, 1914. Commissioned 1914, decommissioned 1939. Served principally on the Yangtze (1914–29), and as lower Yangtze guardship (1929–31). She was the second USS *Monocacy* to serve on the Yangtze.

Palos (PG-16): Commissioned 1914, decommissioned 1937. Reclassified as PR-1 in 1928. Served principally on the Yangtze (1914–28), and as lower Yangtze guardship (1928–34). Served as Chungking guardship on the upper Yangtze (1934–37).

Guam Class

Gunboats in class	2 – Guam (Wake), Tutuila
Displacement	350 tons
Dimensions	Length: 159ft 6in; Beam: 27ft; Draught: 5ft 3in
Power	1,950 steam horsepower
Speed	14½ knots
Armament	Two 3in guns, eight single machine-guns (10 machine-guns from 1938)
Complement	59 officers and men

Guam (PG-43): Launched in Shanghai, 1927. Commissioned 1927, reclassified as PR-3 in 1928 and renamed *Wake* in 1941. Captured by Japanese, 8 December 1941. Served principally on the Yangtze (1927–37) and as Shanghai guardship (1937–41). She served as the IJNS *Tatara* until August 1945, when she was recaptured by the US Navy. She was subsequently handed over to the Chinese Navy, and renamed the *Tai Yuan*. Captured by the Chinese communists in 1949, and remained in service until the 1960s.

Tutuila (PG-44): Commissioned 1928, decommissioned 1937. Reclassified as PR-4 in 1928. Served principally on the Yangtze (1928–38) and as Chungking guardship, on the upper Yangtze (1938–41). Transferred to the Chinese Navy in February 1942, and renamed the *Mei Yuan*. Scuttled off Shanghai in May 1949, to prevent her capture by the Chinese communists.

On 12 December 1937, Japanese aircraft inadvertently attacked the gunboat USS *Panay*, which was lying upriver from Nanking. She was hit by two bombs, and sank in shallow water. Three sailors were killed, and the incident caused outrage in America.

Panay Class

Gunboats in class	2 – *Panay, Oahu*
Displacement	474 tons
Dimensions	Length: 191ft; Beam: 29ft; Draught: 5ft 3in
Power	2,250 steam horsepower
Speed	15 knots
Armament	Two 3in guns, eight single machine-guns (10 machine-guns on Oahu from 1938)
Complement	59 officers and men

Panay (PG-45): Launched in Shanghai, 1927. Commissioned 1928. Reclassified as PR-6 in 1928. Served principally on the Yangtze (1928–37), until sunk by Japanese aircraft off Nanking on 12 December 1937.

Oahu (PG-46): Commissioned 1928. Reclassified as PR-6 in 1928. She served on the Yangtze (1928–37) and as Nanking guardship (1938–41). She was in the Philippines on 7 December 1941, and joined the Asiatic Fleet in Manila Bay, helping to defend the anchorage until she was sunk by gunfire in Manila Bay, 5 May 1942.

Luzon Class

Gunboats in class	2 – *Luzon, Mindanao*
Displacement	560 tons
Dimensions	Length: 211ft; Beam: 31ft; Draught: 5ft 6in
Power	3,150 steam horsepower
Speed	16 knots
Armament	Two 3in guns, eight single machine-guns (10 machine-guns from 1938)
Complement	70 officers and men

Luzon (PG-47): Launched in Shanghai, 1927. Commissioned 1927. Reclassified as PR-7 (1928). Served principally on the Yangtze (1927–38) and as Shanghai guardship (1938–41). She was in the Philippines when the islands were invaded by the Japanese, and was subsequently scuttled in Manila Bay on 6 May 1942. In late 1942 she was raised, and re-commissioned as the IJNS *Karatsu*. She was torpedoed and sunk off the Philippines in March 1944.

Mindanao (PG-48): Commissioned 1928. Reclassified as PR-8 in 1928. She served on the Yangtze (1928–29), but her principal bases were Hong Kong and Canton (1929–41). Following attack on Pearl Harbor, she joined the Asiatic Fleet in Manila Bay, and helped defend the bay until she was bombed and scuttled on 2 May 1942.

BIBLIOGRAPHY

Archibald, E. H. H., *The Fighting Ship in the Royal Navy*, Blandford, Poole (1984)

Brice, Martin H., *The Royal Navy and the Sino–Japanese Incident 1937–41*, Littlehampton Book Services Ltd, London (1973)

Cole, Bernard D., *Gunboats and Marines: The United States Navy in China, 1925–1928* Associated University Presses, Cranbury, NJ (1983)

Earl, Lawrence, *Yangtse Incident: The Story of HMS* Amethyst, George G. Harrap & Co., London (1950)

Gelber, Harry G., *The Dragon and the Foreign Devils: China and the World, 1100 BC to the Present*, Bloomsbury, London (2007)

Guernsey, H. C., *A Naval Career*, Arthur H. Stockwell Ltd, London (1992)

Haines, Gregory, *Gunboats on the Great River*, Macdonald and Jane's, London (1976)

Hampshire, A. Cecil, *Armed with Stings*, William Kimber & Co., London (1958)

Howell, Glen F., *Gunboats on the Yangtze: The Diary of Captain Glen F. Howell of the USS* Palos, 1920–21, McFarland Ltd, Jefferson, NC (2002)

Kemp, Paul J., *Gunboats of the Royal Navy*, ISO Publications, London (1997)

Lyne, Sir Thomas J. Spence, *Something about a Sailor*, Mayflower Press, Plymouth (1940)

Perrett, Bryan, *Gunboat! Small Ships at War*, Cassell, London (2000)

Perry, Hamilton-Derby, *The* Panay *Incident: Prelude to Pearl Harbor*, Macmillan, New York (1967)

Phillips, C. E. Lucas, *The Escape of the* Amethyst, Heinemann, London (1957)

Preston, Antony & Major, John, *Send a Gunboat: The Victorian Navy and at Sea, 1854–1904*, Conway Maritime Press, London (2007)

Pugsley, A. F., *Destroyer Man*, Weidenfeld & Nicholson, London (1957)

Tolley, Kemp, *Yangtze Patrol: The US Navy in China*, Naval Institute Press, Annapolis, MD (2000)

One of the smallest gunboats in China was the Portuguese *Macao*, a vessel that was based in the Portuguese-run treaty port (now Macao) that shared her name, although she occasionally flew the flag in Shanghai. She was decommissioned in 1942.

INDEX

Page numbers in **bold** refer to illustrations and plates